ICONS

Dessous

Dessous

Lingerie as Erotic Weapon

Gilles Néret

TASCHEN

KÖLN LONDON MADRID NEW YORK PARIS TOKYO

The Venus Fly-trap

Women's lingerie is the stuff of fantasy. A vital element in the skilled art of undressing, it never fails to work its strange magic on the libido. The sexual organs are prosaic unless seen through a veil that emphasises their forbidden attractions. In the words of Montaigne (1533–1592): "Some things are best displayed by concealment." Women have worn underwear since the dawn of civilisation, sometimes openly, sometimes secretly, as the social climate dictated. Society frequently advanced hypocritical pretexts for wearing lingerie, invoking dubious reasons of health and hygiene. No one was willing to admit that these clinging undergarments, these "snares of Venus", actually clothed the erotic life of eras perverse, brutal or more refined. In so doing, they satisfied the fantasies of the women who wore these diabolical contraptions and the men who were aroused by them. Ribbons, petticoats, corsets, drawers, brassieres, knickers, silk stockings, nylons and suspender-belts have all played their part in the mysterious pas de deux that has united men and women since time immemorial.

Lingerie is an essential prop in the passion play performed by men and women. The lights go down, the curtain rises like a skirt to reveal an indecorous décor of lingerie and the show begins; this is a performance that may well continue later behind closed doors. Although complete nudity might be acceptable for statues, the fetishist appeal of lingerie can add spice to any appetite. According to Magnus Hirschfeld (1868–1935), of 1,000 men surveyed, only 350 were attracted to wholly naked women; 400 men preferred them in a partial state of undress and 250 showed a marked preference for fully-clothed women. In other words, 65% of men displayed fetishist tendencies. There is no doubt that sexy underwear affords endless potential for the woman who enjoys the act of seduction. We seem to hear the voice of Faust crying out in an ecstasy of love: "Bring me a fichu that has covered her breast, a ribbon that belongs to my love!". The epic history of lingerie, from its origins to the height of its glory in film and advertising, illustrates how women have always treated the need to wear clothes and the desire to take them off as a pretext for enhancing their feminine allure.

The two earliest undergarments for women date back to 2000 BC in Crete: the crinoline and the corset. However, Cretan women, variously described by historians as "dolls" or "magnificent sluts", merely wore these figure-hugging garments to lift and accentuate their bare breasts or emphasise their hips, making their bodies seem more voluptuous and desirable. Lingerie has the power to reverse roles so that the defenceless fisherman takes the bait and is reeled in by the beautiful fish. As the myth goes, it was none other than Venus who invented the first embroidered corset, the cestus, that sheathed the body from the groin to the base of the breasts, making it appear more slender. It is said that she strongly recommended this garment to Juno, a goddess with an overly curvaceous figure, in a bid to keep Zeus, her fickle husband, from straying. Martial (c. 40–c. 104) described it as a snare from which no man could escape, a device perfectly suited to rekindling the flames of love; he himself was aroused by the thought of touching a cestus "still warm from Venus's fire". Women, programmed by nature to arouse men's desire and so save the human race from extinction, soon realised that they could only fulfil this vital function and incite men to acts of passion by giving free rein to their own passion for underwear, thereby accentuating the natural differences between the sexes. Women selected their lingerie to serve as a continual reminder to their lovers that they were indeed a breed apart. As soon as one style of lingerie lost its appeal, another took its place, ensuring that a man had far more exciting things on his mind than sleep.

After the fat years come the lean years, so they say, and this loose-fitting style of dress was soon replaced by an extremely restrictive fashion. By 1900, women's clothes were more restrictive than ever. A woman's assignation with her lover between 5pm and 7pm took longer and longer because he had to remove her massive corset, a true instrument of torture stretching from her shoulders to her thighs – how lingerie brings out the masochist in women! – followed by her long chemise, an under-bodice, drawers and countless petticoats. All these garments were guarded by numerous buttons and bristling with murderous fasteners, making this thorny rose a dangerous flower to pluck. Certainly, peeling this onion could reduce a strong man to tears. This almost impregnable barrage of lingerie, which also served as an incitement to debauchery, initially gave rise to foot and ankle fetishes since there was little else to be seen of the Art Nouveau woman. However, with the birth of striptease, the slow and involved act of undressing became a performance, an art at which the Americans soon excelled. In Paris, the first spectators of this new form of entertainment were contemporaries of Toulouse-Lautrec and his friends, who went to see many performances of the "Coucher d'Yvette" (Yvette's Bedtime Routine) and were delighted on the frequent occasions that the French Cancan dancers did not wear any knickers.

▶ François Boucher: *The Toilet* (detail) · *Die Morgentoilette* (Detail) · *La Toilette* (détail). 1742

The Vamp, in the manner of Marlene Dietrich in the Blue Angel, used black silk stockings and a suspender belt to devastating effect. Pin-up girls, epitomised by Hollywood movie stars like Ava Gardner, Rita Hayworth or Jean Harlow, continued to make good use of these deadly weapons to the great joy of the American GIs fighting in the Pacific, who proudly pinned photos of these scantily-dressed women to the walls of their barracks. Since then, pin-up girls have invaded all areas of society, from films, the tabloid press and the advertising industry to the world of sadomasochism. Modelling themselves on Marilyn Monroe or Brigitte Bardot, they once promoted deodorants, cars or dishwashers. The modern-day pin-up, far from the amoral, carefree grisette at the turn of the 20th century, who was approachable, harmless and concerned only with her plumes, poses and lovers, has become more aggressive. This is the all-American Superwoman or Supervixen with her specialised packaging of provocative lingerie, a product of sexual pop art, the "living currency" of the consumer society. She has gradually been kitted out with boots, whips and a barbed bra.

Fortunately, these extravagant items of underwear remain playthings enabling people to enjoy themselves in the privacy of their own homes or in clubs, to organise provocative shows and indulge in an infinite variety of harmless sexual entertainments. After all, wearing lingerie is governed more than ever by instinct and sensitivity, essentially feminine qualities. Now that wearing tights is the norm, the woman who, on certain evenings, still puts on her now redundant suspender-belt can expect to make a certain impact. She is a new type of romantic: liberated from the clichéd view of the woman as sex slave, she knows that her conscious attitude has a significance for her and for others. This deliberate choice has become a special bond between the woman who wears it and the man who has access to it.

Anyone who loves women and knows a little about their intimate personal relationship with lingerie, cannot help joining Jacques Laurent in his plea: "Because lingerie clings to the most secret, the most febrile and, for men, the most thrilling parts of a woman's body… it allows the imagination to run riot. Women may be running a risk if they forget that lingerie is a unique weapon because it is designed to please the man it strikes while arousing in him the desire to strike back".

◄ Eugène Atget: *Corsets on the Boulevard de Strasbourg · Korsettgeschäft am Boulevard de Strasbourg. · Corsets boulevard de Strasbourg.* 1909
►► The dance number from *French Can-Can* by Jean Renoir · Ballettszene aus „French Cancan" von Jean Renoir · Le ballet de « French cancan », de Jean Renoir. 1955

Die Venusfalle

Dessous verführen zum Träumen. Sie üben eine eigenartige Macht auf die Libido aus und sind sowohl Requisite als auch Zauberformel raffinierter Entkleidungskunst. Denn was ist ein nackter Körper ohne jeglichen Schmuck, ohne den Reiz des Verbotenen? „Gewisse Dinge versteckt man, um sie zu zeigen", sagte schon Montaigne (1533–1592). Seit Anbeginn der Zivilisation begleitet Damenunterwäsche die Geschichte der Menschheit. In Zeiten des Überflusses blieb sie im Verborgenen, in Zeiten des Umbruchs hingegen zeigte sie sich üppig und verwegen. Um ihren Gebrauch zu rechtfertigen, berief man sich stets heuchlerisch auf ihre angebliche Schutz- und Hygienefunktion. In Wahrheit sollte nur nicht an die große Glocke gehängt werden, daß diese „zweite Haut", diese „Venusfalle" eine höchst perverse, je nach Epoche brutale oder subtile Erotik bediente, also die Phantasien beider Seiten befriedigte – derjenigen, die dieses Teufelsgerät anlegten, und derjenigen, die es mit Lust enthüllten. Strumpfbänder, Unterröcke, Korsetts, Pantalons, Büstenhalter und Schlüpfer reihten sich nacheinander ein in den geheimnisvollen Reigen, der den Mann seit jeher mit der Weiblichkeit vereint.

 Dessous dürfen bei der Inszenierung des Theaterstücks, in dem Männer und Frauen die Hauptrollen spielen, nicht fehlen. Das Klingelzeichen ertönt, der Vorhang hebt sich wie ein Rock, das Dessous erscheint als Dekor auf der Bühne und das Spektakel beginnt, um gegebenenfalls in der Intimität des Schlafzimmers fortgesetzt zu werden. Denn während die totale Nacktheit für Statuen angemessen ist, verleiht der Verhüllungsfetischismus jedem Festmahl erst die notwendige Würze. Laut Magnus Hirschfeld (1868–1935) fühlen sich von 1000 Männern nur 350 von einem völlig nackten Frauenkörper angezogen, 400 finden halbbekleidete und 250 der Befragten vollständig bekleidete Frauen sexuell attraktiv. Mit anderen Worten, 65% der männlichen Bevölkerung hegen fetischistische Neigungen. Erinnern wir uns daran, was Faust im Liebesrausch ruft: „Schafft mir ein Halstuch von ihrer Brust, ein Strumpfband meiner Liebeslust!" Von den Anfängen bis zu seiner Blütezeit in Film und Werbung erzählt das Epos des Dessous, wie die Notwendigkeit sich zu verhüllen oder die Lust sich zu enthüllen, Eva und ihren Töchtern zu allen Zeiten als Vorwand diente, ihre Weiblichkeit und Erotik in Szene zu setzen.

◄ The simple, provocative works of an American fetishist photographer, Elmer Batters, alias "Mr Black Silk Stockings", also called "Mr Foot" due to his other obsession · Die naiven und zugleich erregenden Fotos des amerikanischen Fetischfotografen Elmer Batters alias „Mr. Black Silk Stockings", auch „Monsieur Pied" genannt wegen seiner speziellen Obsession · Les œuvres naïves et émouvantes d'un photographe fétichiste américain, Elmer Batters, alias « Mr. Black Silk Stockings », dit aussi « Monsieur Pied » pour son obsession particulière... 1960s. In Elmer Batters. *From the tip of the toes to the top of the hose.* Taschen. 1995

Die ersten beiden Dessous, das Korsett und ein Volantrock, der einen ähnlichen Effekt erzielte wie später die Krinoline, eroberten Kreta bereits 2000 Jahre v. Chr. Doch die kretische Frau, von Elie Faure als „Puppe", von Jacques Laurent als „herrliches Luder" bezeichnet, benutzte die beiden Kleidungsstücke lediglich, um ihre Brüste zu heben und üppiger erscheinen zu lassen und um ihre Taille zu betonen, also ihren Körper kurvenreicher zu gestalten. Das Dessous besitzt also die Macht, die Rollen zu vertauschen: es ist der hübsche Fisch, der mit Hilfe seines Köders den wehrlosen Fischer fängt. Nach der Mythologie soll der Cestus, eine Art verziertes Korsett, das von der Leiste bis unter den Busen reicht, von Venus persönlich entworfen worden sei, und sie empfahl ihn wärmstens der etwas in die Breite gegangenen Juno. Martial (40–104 n. Chr.) nennt den Cestus eine Falle, der kein Mann entkommen kann, den Köder par excellence, der die Liebesflamme wieder neu entfacht; er selbst geriet in heftige Erregung, als er mit einem Cestus in Berührung kam, der „noch heiß von den Feuern der Venus" war.

Die Frauen haben also schon sehr früh begriffen, daß sie nur zum Objekt der Begierde werden konnten, indem sie sich in puncto Dessous befreiten und die biologischen Unterschiede, die sie in den Augen der Männer so fremdartig machten, hervorhoben. Mit Hilfe des Dessous konnten sie ihre Liebhaber fortwährend daran erinnern, daß sie anderen Geschlechts waren.

So wie ein fetter Papst auf einen mageren folgt, wechselt sich die freizügige Mode mit einer zugeknöpften ab. Nie zuvor wurde die Frau so verschnürt und verriegelt wie um 1900. Die Frau war eingeschnürt in ein riesiges Korsett, von den Brüsten bis zu den Schenkeln (ein wahres Folterinstrument, eines ausgewachsenen Sadomasochisten würdig), und darüber trug sie ein langes Hemd, ein cache-corset, eine Unterhose und mehrere Unterröcke. Es dauerte Stunden, diese Zwiebel aus ihren Häuten zu schälen. Dieser bis zum Rand mit Verboten, aber auch mit virtuellen Verführungen zur Unzucht gefüllte Dampfkessel musste bald explodieren. Zunächst aber rief er die Fuß- und Stiefelettenfetischisten auf den Plan, da im Jugendstil mehr von den Frauen nicht zu erhaschen war. Mit der Erfindung des Striptease jedoch entwickelte sich das aufwändige Herausschälen zu einer wahren Kunst, welche die Amerikaner schon bald meisterhaft beherrschten. Ihre ersten Bewunderer waren allerdings die Zeitgenossen von Toulouse-Lautrec und seinen Freunden, die mit Vorliebe diverse „Coucher d'Yvette" aufsuchten und begeistert feststellten, dass die Tänzerinnen des French Cancan die Freundlichkeit besaßen, des Öfteren auf Unterhosen zu verzichten.

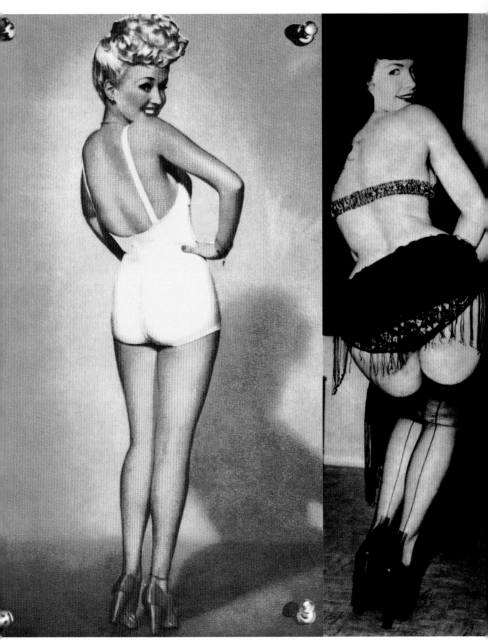

The first pin-up: Betty Grable. Her legs were insured for a million dollars · Das erste Pin-up mit Reißzwecken. Betty Grable ließ sich ihre Beine für eine Million Dollar versichern. · La première Pin-up, avec ses punaises... Betty Grable et ses jambes assurées pour un million de dollars... 1942.

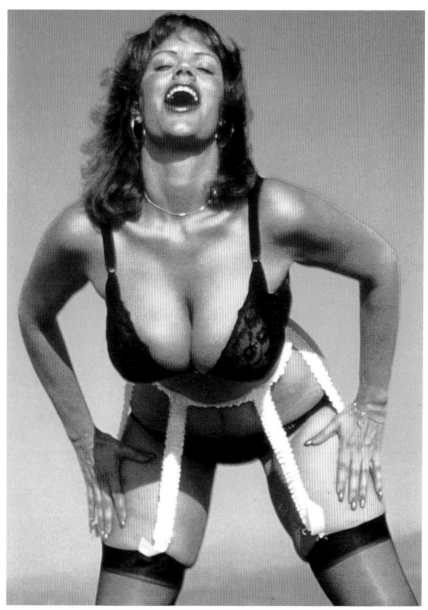

"Supervixen" (championed by Russ Meyer, who favoured pneumatic breasts and belligerent thighs), set the trend for the intrepid lingerie worn by superwomen of the future · „SUPERVIXEN" – wie Russ Meyer sie bevorzugt, der Liebhaber von Riesenbrüsten und strammen Schenkeln – preisen die Superdessous der Superfrau von morgen an… · « SUPERVIXEN » (chère à Russ Meyer, le chantre des poitrines triomphantes et des cuisses guerrières), annonce les super-dessous de la super-femme de demain…

Der Vamp vom Typ Marlene Dietrich in „Der blaue Engel" erklärt schwarze Seidenstrümpfe und Strumpfhaltergürtel zu seinen Lieblingswaffen, die er an seine Nachfolgerin, das amerikanische „Pin-up" weitervererbt. Hollywood-Stars von Ava Gardner bis Rita Hayworth und Jean Harlow machen reichlich Gebrauch davon – zur großen Freude der G.I.s, die im Pazifik kämpfen und stolz ihre freizügigen Fotos an die Lagerwände pinnen.

Von da an setzt sich der Siegeszug der Pin-ups vom Kino bis zur Boulevardpresse, von der Werbung bis zur Sado-Maso-Szene in alle Bereiche fort. Inspiriert durch Marilyn Monroe oder Brigitte Bardot, preist das Pin-up ein Deo, ein Auto oder eine Waschmaschine an. Weit entfernt von der amoralischen, unbekümmerten Grisette zu Anfang des Jahrhunderts, die einzig um ihre Federn, ihre Posen und ihre Liebhaber besorgt war, wird das Pin-up made in USA zunehmend aggressiv. Als Superwoman oder Supervixen wird es mit Hilfe einer passenden Dessousverpackung in Szene gesetzt, ist Gegenstand der Sex-Popart und „lebendes Geld" der Konsumgesellschaft. Nach und nach rüstet es sich mit Stiefeln, Peitsche und Spitz-BH. Zum Glück handelt es sich hierbei noch immer um Spielzeuge, die es erlauben, sich zu Hause oder im Club zu amüsieren und unbesorgt teuflisch scharfe Vorstellungen mit endlos variierbaren Sexualpraktiken zu inszenieren. Denn das Dessous fällt mehr denn je in den Bereich von Instinkt und Empfindsamkeit, beides urweibliche Eigenschaften ... Auch im Zeitalter der Strumpfhose legt manche Frau an besonderen Abenden noch immer den eigentlich unnützen Strumpfhaltergürtel an, weil sie sich davon das gewünschte Maß an Aufregung verspricht. Sie verkörpert den neuen Typ der Romantikerin, befreit vom Klischee der Sklavin, die sich im Gegenteil der Bedeutung, die dieser willentliche Akt für sie selbst und ihr Gegenüber hat, völlig bewusst ist. Der Strumpfhaltergürtel ist heute ein privilegiertes Bindeglied zwischen derjenigen, die sich damit schmückt und demjenigen, der Zugang dazu hat.

Und all jene, die Frauen lieben und ein wenig von ihrer ganz eigenen Beziehung zu Dessous verstehen, können nicht umhin, in den Lobgesang Jacques Laurents einzustimmen: „Das Dessous, Wächter der geheimsten, aufregendsten Stellen einer Frau, jene, die dem Mann den Atem rauben... verführt als Spielball der Phantasie die Frau zu manch einem Wagnis; oft vergisst sie dabei, dass das Dessous vor allem eine unschlagbare Waffe ist – unschlagbar, weil sie dazu bestimmt ist, demjenigen, den sie aufstachelt, zu gefallen, indem sie den Stachel in ihm weckt".

▶▶ Fantasy in uniform, or naughty nurses on parade · Das wild gewordene Krankenhaus. · Le fantasme de l'uniforme, ou l'hôpital en folie... In *Lui,* the French *Playboy* of the 1980s.

GAINES * CEINTURES * SOUTIEN-GORGE

Delmotte: Scandale *girdle,* or Eve and the serpent · *Hüfthalter* „Scandale" oder Eva und die Schlange · La *gaine* «
Scandale» ou Eve et le serpent... 1947

Le Piège de Vénus

Les dessous féminins sont avant tout des «supports de rêve». Ils possèdent sur la libido un étrange pouvoir. Ils sont à la pièce maîtresse de l'art du déshabillé savant et sa formule magique. Le sexe, en effet, n'est rien sans la parure, sans les séductions de l'interdit. «Il y a certaines choses que l'on cache pour les montrer», disait déjà Montaigne (1533–1592). Depuis les débuts de la civilisation, les dessous féminins ont accompagné l'histoire de l'humanité. Tantôt ils prolifèrent, selon les périodes fastes ou les périodes troublées. On a fait régulièrement appel à la protection qu'ils sont supposés apporter et à l'hygiène qu'ils n'assurent pas forcément pour en justifier l'usage. En réalité, ce que l'on préfère passer sous silence, c'est que cette «seconde peau», ce «piège de Vénus», répond le plus souvent à l'érotisme le plus pervers, agressif ou subtil selon les époques et les pays, assouvissant ainsi les fantasmes, aussi bien de celles qui ont choisi de porter ces engins diaboliques, que de ceux qui les découvrent avec émotion. Rubans, jupons, corsets, pantalons, soutiens-gorge, petites culottes, bas de soie ou de nylon, porte-jarretelles ont participé tour à tour à cette ronde mystérieuse qui a toujours uni l'homme à la féminité.

Les dessous sont essentiels à la mise en scène d'une pièce de théâtre dont l'homme et la femme sont les acteurs. On frappe les trois coups, le rideau se lève comme une jupe, le décor des dessous apparaît et le spectacle commence qui peut se prolonger dans l'intimité de l'alcôve. Car si la nudité totale vaut pour les statues, le fétichisme de la parure apporte les condiments nécessaires à tout festin. D'après Magnus Hirschfeld (1868–1935), sur 1000 hommes, 350 seulement sont attirés par le corps de la femme entièrement nu tandis que 400 le préfèrent à moitié déshabillé et que 250 ont une attirance marquée pour qu'il reste vêtu. En d'autres termes, 65% des individus masculins ont des tendances fétichistes. On voit l'étendue des possibilités qu'offrent les dessous révélateurs à la femme qui veut séduire. Qu'on se souvienne de Faust s'écriant dans un bel élan d'amour: «Apportez-moi un fichu, qui ait couvert son sein, un ruban de ma bien aimée!» Des débuts de son histoire jusqu'à l'apogée du cinéma et de la publicité, l'épopée des dessous illustre comment, de tous temps, le besoin de se couvrir ou l'envie de se découvrir a été pour Eve et ses descendantes prétexte à mettre en valeur sa féminité et son pouvoir érotique.

C'est en Crète, 2000 ans av. J.-C., que l'on découvre les deux premiers dessous spécifiques de la femme: la crinoline et le corset. Mais déjà la Crétoise, que les historiens traitent tantôt de «poupée» ou de «garce superbe», ne s'en sert que pour rendre ses seins nus plus arrogants en les pressant à la base, ou pour accentuer ses hanches et rendre son corps plus épanoui, plus désirable. Les dessous ont ainsi le pouvoir d'inverser les rôles et c'est le joli poisson qui par ses leurres attrape le pauvre pêcheur... Selon la mythologie, c'est Vénus elle-même qui aurait inventé la première gaine, le cestus, qui enveloppait le corps de ses broderies depuis l'aine jusqu'à la base des seins et l'amincissait, cestus dont elle conseillait vivement l'usage à Junon, un peu trop épanouie, pour retenir Zeus, son volage époux. Martial (v. 40–v.104), en parle comme d'un piège auquel aucun homme ne peut échapper, comme l'appât par excellence qui peut ranimer la flamme amoureuse, et lui-même s'émeut au contact d'un cestus «encore tout chaud des feux de Vénus».

C'est donc très tôt que les femmes, programmées par la nature pour provoquer le désir des hommes, sans quoi l'humanité serait appelée à disparaître, ont compris qu'elles ne pouvaient assumer leur rôle essentiel et devenir l'objet de passion qu'en se déchaînant en matière de dessous pour accentuer les différences naturelles qui les faisaient étrangères aux hommes. Les dessous étant pour elles une façon de rappeler sans cesse à leurs amants qu'elles étaient d'une race autre. Dès qu'une recette cesse son effet, aussitôt une autre vient la remplacer et réveiller les ardeurs du mâle trop enclin au sommeil.

Comme les papes gras, dit-on, succèdent aux papes maigres, la mode carcérale succède à la mode ouverte à tous les vents. Jamais la femme n'a été aussi prisonnière qu'en 1900. Ses rendez-vous de 5 à 7 avec son amant s'allongent tant il est difficile de la dépouiller successivement de son gigantesque corset, véritable instrument de torture sado-masochiste qui la comprime des épaules aux cuisses – mais la femme adore souffrir dès lors qu'il s'agit de dessous – puis de lui ôter sa longue chemise, son cache-corset, son pantalon, ses multiples jupons, tous accessoires défendus par d'innombrables boutons, hérissés d'agrafes assassines qui font de cette rose à épines une dangereuse fleur et un oignon qu'il faut des heures pour éplucher. Cette marmite bourrée d'interdits mais aussi d'incitations virtuelles à la débauche, va bientôt exploser, donnant d'abord naissance aux fétichistes du pied et de la bottine, puisque c'est tout ce que l'on peut voir de la femme du style nouille. Mais ce difficile épluchage devient aussi un art avec l'invention du «strip-tease», dont les Américains deviendront les maîtres, mais dont les premiers spectateurs sont les contemporains de Toulouse-Lautrec et ses amis, enchantés d'assister aux divers «Coucher d'Yvette» et ravis de constater que les danseuses du French-Cancan ont la gentillesse d'omettre souvent d'enfiler un pantalon.

Stockings promotion in a New York department store · Werbung für *Strümpfe* in einem New Yorker Warenhaus ·
Publicité pour des bas dans un grand magasin new-yorkais. 1950s

Jean Paul
GAULTIER

PARFUMS

La Vamp, du type Marlene Dietrich dans «L'Ange bleu», va s'emparer des bas de soie noire et du porte-jarretelles pour en faire ses armes favorites. Armes qu'elle transmettra à la «pin-up» qui va lui succéder et qui, incarnée par les stars d'Hollywood, d'Ava Gardner à Rita Hayworth ou Jean Harlow, en fera bon usage à la grande joie des G.I.'s en train de se battre dans le Pacifique et fiers d'épingler leurs photos dénudées sur les murs de leur campement. Désormais la pin-up va envahir tous les domaines, du cinéma à la presse légère et de la publicité au sado-masochisme. Lorsqu'elle s'inspirait encore de Marilyn Monroe ou de Brigitte Bardot, c'était pour mieux vanter gentiment un déodorant, une automobile ou un lave-vaisselle. Aujourd'hui, bien loin de la grisette amorale et insouciante du début du siècle, accessive et sans danger, uniquement soucieuse de ses plumes, de ses poses, de ses amants, la pin-up made in USA, est devenue agressive. C'est Superwoman ou Supervixen, mise en valeur par un emballage de dessous ad-hoc, issue du pop-art sexuel, «monnaie vivante» de la société de consommation. Peu à peu elle se harnache de bottes et de fouets et son soutien-gorge se couvre de piquants.

Heureusement, ces exagérations restent des jouets permettant de s'amuser en privé ou en club, d'organiser des spectacles épicés en diable et d'effectuer sans danger des performance sexuelles variées à l'infini. Car le dessous reste plus que jamais du domaine de l'instinct et de la sensibilité, qualités essentiellements féminines… A l'ère du collant, celle qui met encore certains soirs un porte-jarretelles devenu totalement inutile, en attend à coup sûr quelques émotions. C'est une romantique d'un nouveau genre, libérée des clichés de femme-esclave et consciente au contraire que son attitude délibérée a une signification pour elle et pour l'autre. Ce choix délibéré est devenu un lien privilégié entre celle qui s'en pare et celui qui y aura accès. Et tous ceux qui aiment la femme et connaissent un peu le secret de ses rapports personnels avec ses dessous, ne peuvent, comme Jacques Laurent, que lui adresser cette prière: «Le dessous, parce qu'il adhère aux régions du corps féminins qui sont les plus secrètes, les plus fiévreuses et pour l'homme les plus dramatiques… L'imagination le gouverne et les femmes prendraient un risque en oubliant qu'il est surtout une arme incomparable parce qu'elle a pour vocation de plaire à celui qu'elle frappe, en lui donnant le désir de frapper.»

◄ Jean-Paul Gaultier uses a retro-style *corset* to sell his perfume · Jean-Paul Gaultier bedient sich des altmodischen *Korsetts*, um sein Parfüm zu verkaufen… · Jean-Paul Gaultier fait appel à un *corset* rétro pour vendre son parfum…
1997
►► Photo of underwear by Elmer Batters · Dessous-Foto von Elmer Batters · Photo de dessous par Elmer Batters.
1960s

TO BENEDIKT
BEST REGARDS

The first *corset* – designed to accentuate Cretan women's proud breasts – and the first *crinoline* – which served only to emphasise their hips · Das erste *Korsett*, das die Brüste der Kreterinnen besser zur Geltung bringen sollte, und die erste Krinoline, die die Hüften betonte · *Le premier corset* – conçu pour rendre les seins de la Crétoise plus arrogants – et *la première crinoline* – destinée à accentuer ses hanches sans autre fonction pratique. Crete. 2000–1700 BC.

Another of Hollywood's early sex symbols, Mae West. Here, in *Diamond Lil* · Ein weiteres Sexsymbol aus den Anfängen Hollywoods, Mae West. Hier ein Standfoto aus „Diamantenlilly" · Autre «sex symbol» des débuts d'Hollywood, Mae West. Ici, dans «Diamond Lil». 1928

Theda Bara, Hollywood's first sex-goddess, in her oriental underwear in *Cleopatra* · Theda Bara, die erste „Sex-Göttin" Hollywoods, zeigt im Film „Cleopatra" ihre orientalischen Dessous · Theda Bara, la première «sex-goddess» d'Hollywood, portant ses dessous orientaux, dans «Cleopatra». 1917

Most Egyptian women wore nothing under their veils or tunics. However, slaves, dancing girls and prostitutes wore a tiny *G-string* (left: Tomb of Djeserkaresonb, Thebes). Women athletes wore the precursor of the *bikini* (Mosaics from a Roman villa. Below right: Atalanta wearing the *first modern undergarment*.) Circa 1400–500 BC

Die Ägypterinnen sind unter ihren Schleiern und Tuniken nackt, nur die Sklavinnen, Tänzerinnen und Prostituierten tragen einen winzigen Lendenschurz (links: Grab des Djeserkaraseneb, Theben), aber auch Sportlerinnen tragen einen Vorgänger des Bikinis (Mosaiken aus einer römischen Villa. Unten rechts: Atalante trägt *das erste moderne Dessous*). Ca. 1400–500 v. Ch.

Les Egyptiennes sont nues sous leurs voiles et leurs tuniques, sauf les esclaves, les danseuses et les prostituées qui portent un infime *cachesexe* (à gauche : Tombe de Djeserkaraseneb, Thèbes), ou les sportives qui portent l'ancêtre du Bikini (Mosaïques d'une villa romaine. En bas à droite : Atalante portant *le premier dessous moderne*). v. 1400–500 av. J.-C.

▲ La Goulue. 1887
◄ Toulouse-Lautrec: *Casual Conquest* (detail), woman wearing a corset for *Elles* · *Flüchtige Eroberung* (Detail), Frau im Korsett für „Elles" · *Conquête de passage* (détail), femme en corset pour « Elles ». 1896

◄ Grille d'égout ▲ Rayon d'Or
►► The famous "5 demi-vierges" · Die berühmten „5 Halbjungfrauen" · Les célèbres « 5 demi-vierges ». C. 1890

Clients waiting in the brothels or luxury whorehouses were given albums of sexy photographs, showing the prostitutes "amusing themselves" · In den Freudenhäusern oder Luxusbordellen gibt man den Kunden zum Zeitvertreib freizügige Fotoalben, die die Freudenmädchen bei ihren privaten Spielen zeigen... · Dans les maisons closes, ou bordels de luxe, pour faire patienter le client, on lui donne à feuilleter des albums de photos licencieuses, montrant les pensionnaires dans leurs ébats privés...

Chained beauties · Die Schönheiten in Ketten · Les belles enchaînées, in *L'Etude Académique*. 1895

▲ Postcard · Postkarte · Carte postale. 1900

▲ *Mirror, Mirror.* Postcard · „Die Schöne im Spiegel," Postkarte · «Joli miroir…», carte postale. 1900   **40 · 41**

▲ With *knickers*. Postcard · Mit *Höschen*... Postkarte · Avec *culotte*... Carte postale. 1900
▶ The revelations of *drawers* at half mast... Postcard · Was die *Unterhose* sonst verhüllt... Postkarte ·
Les révélations du *pantalon* qui tombe... Carte postale. 1900

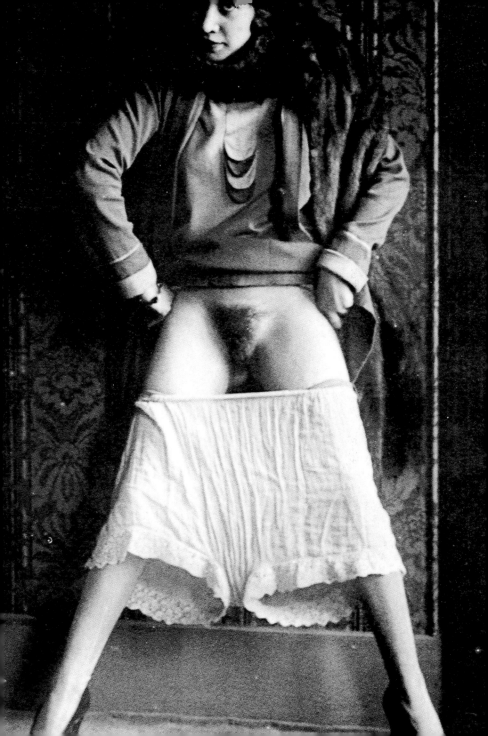

Honoré Daumier: *Outside the Corset-makers.* "Well I never, there's my wife!" · *Vor dem Korsettgeschäft.* „Sieh da, meine Frau…" · *Devant le magazin de corsets.* « Tiens voilà ma femme… ». 1840

American maternity corset. · Amerikanisches Korsett für Schwangere und stillende Mütter · *Corset* de grossesse et d'allaitement américain. 1908

The *corset* worn for cycling · Das passende Korsett zum Fahrradfahren · Le *corset* pour faire de la bicyclette. Photo from *Die Erotik in der Photographie*. 1898

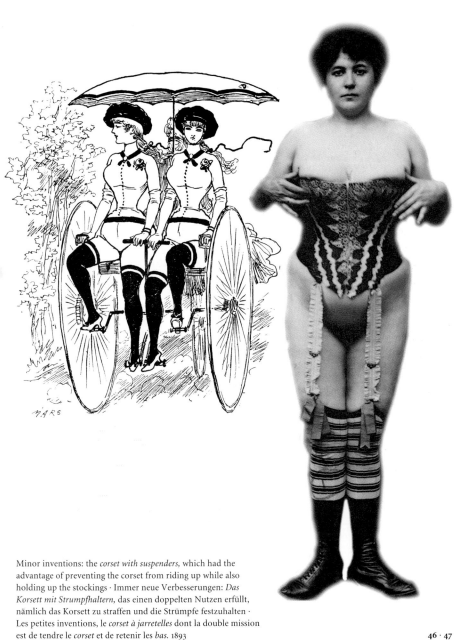

Minor inventions: the *corset with suspenders*, which had the
advantage of preventing the corset from riding up while also
holding up the stockings · Immer neue Verbesserungen: *Das
Korsett mit Strumpfhaltern*, das einen doppelten Nutzen erfüllt,
nämlich das Korsett zu straffen und die Strümpfe festzuhalten ·
Les petites inventions, le *corset à jarretelles* dont la double mission
est de tendre le *corset* et de retenir les *bas*. 1893

▲ The wasp-waist. · Die „Wespentaille" · La «taille de guêpe». C. 1893
◀ Eugène Atget: *The Crinoline Shop* · *Das Krinolinengeschäft* · *La boutique de crinolines*. C. 1880

x

48 · 49

▲ The art of lacing or unlacing *the "Sylphide" corset* · Wie man sein Sylphidenkorsett zu- und wieder aufschnürt ·
L'art de lacer et de délacer son *corset Sylphide*. C. 1900
▶ Raphaël Kirchner: *The Elegant Corset* (Salon des humoristes) · *Das modische Korsett* (Salon der Humoristen) ·
Le corset chic (Salon des humoristes). C. 1900

▲ Edith la Sylphe, the monologuiste · Edith la Sylphe, eine „Diseuse" · Une « diseuse », Edith la Sylphe
► Her instrument, *the "Sylphide" corset* · Ihre wichtigste Requisite, das *Korsett Sylphide* · Son instrument, *le corset Sylphide.* C. 1900

French Belle-Epoque jewellers designed a dazzling array of bejewelled *bras, garters* studded with precious stones, and a new generation of *knickers* and *chastity belts* made of precious metals and gems · Die Juweliere der Belle Epoque kreieren einen ausschweifenden *Büstenhalter* aus Edelsteinen, *Strumpfbänder* aus Diamanten, *Höschen* und *Keuschheitsgürtel* ganz neuen Stils aus Edelmetallen und Edelsteinen · Les joailliers de la Belle Epoque créent une débauche de *soutien-gorges* en pierreries, de *jarretières* de diamants, de *culottes* et de *ceintures de chasteté* d'un nouveau genre, en métal fin et en pierres précieuses.

▲ La Belle Otéro and her *suspender belt* made in precious stones by the jeweller Boucheron during the reign of Napoleon III · Die Schöne Otero mit ihrem Strumpfhalter aus Edelsteinen, gearbeitet zur Zeit Napoleons III. vom Juwelier Boucheron · La Belle Otéro et son *porte-jarretelles* en pierres précieuses, réalisé sous Napoléon III par le joaillier Boucheron. ►► Typical lingerie and inevitable cloche hat worn by women in 1925 · Die klassischen Dessous und der unvermeidliche Glockenhut der Frau um 1925 · Les dessous classiques et le chapeau-cloche obligatoire de la femme 1925.

Women's fashion during the Roaring Twenties: *stockings* and *négligée,* along with the inevitable cloche hat · Moderichtung für die Frau der wilden Zwanziger: *Strümpfe* und *Negligés*... Natürlich nicht ohne den unvermeidlichen Glockenhut · La tenue générale de la femme des Années Folles : *bas* et *déshabillés*... sans oublier l'inévitable chapeau-cloche.

In the 1920s–30s, photographers from Brassaï to Man Ray made their anonymous debuts with photos for erotic post-cards or girlie magazines · In den 20er bis 30er Jahren haben berühmte Fotografen von Brassaï bis Man Ray sich ano-nym im Metier der erotischen Postkarte und des frivolen Magazins versucht · Dans les années 20–30, les plus grands photographes, de Brassaï à Man Ray, ont débuté anonymement dans la carte postale érotique ou le magazine léger.

"Off to the bidet with you, ladies"... at a time when the bidet, with its removable cover, still resembled a chair · „Aufs Bidet, meine Damen..." – als das Bidet noch wie ein Stuhl aussah und einen abnehmbaren Deckel besaß ·

«Au bidet, Mesdames...» à une époque où le bidet ressemblait encore à une chaise, avec couvercle amovible...
1920s

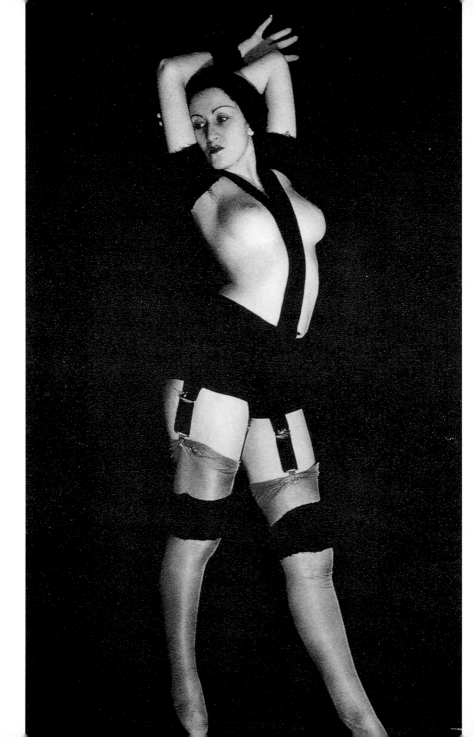

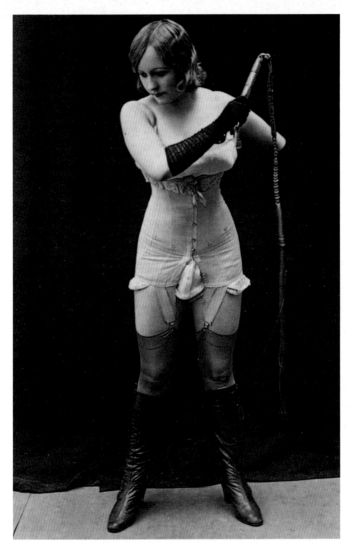

▲Sadomasochistic depravity in the Roaring Twenties: whips, padlocked *G-strings,* and *garters* or *suspenders* that re-semble chains · Die SM-Verworfenheit der wilden Zwanziger: Peitschen, Vorhängeschlösser als *cache-sexe, Strumpf-bänder* und *Strapse,* die aussehen wie Ketten... · Les turpitudes sado-maso des Années Folles... Avec fouets, cadenas en guise de *cache-sexe* et *jarretières* ou *jarretelles* qui évoquent des chaînes...

◄ An outfit half-way between surrealism and bondage · Eine Aufmachung zwischen Surrealismus und Bondage · Un harnachement à mi-chemin entre le surréalisme et le bondage. Photographed by Man Ray. 1929

►► Anonymous, *The Punishment,* or SM in schools. Although taken in the 1920s, the photo has an old-fashioned feel, due to the extremely practical divided drawers · Anonym: „Die Bestrafung" oder Der Sadomasochismus in der Schule. Das Foto wurde in den 20er Jahren aufgenommen, wirkt aber sehr viel älter, wenn man die geschlitzten Unterhosen betrachtet · Anonyme, «La Punition», ou le sado-maso à l'école. Bien que faite dans les années 20, la photo prend un air rétro, grâce aux pantalons fendus...

The *corset* also became retro in style, worn by dominant women · Das *Korsett* wird zum nostalgischen Utensil für „starke" Frauen · Le *corset* devient aussi rétro, pour femmes dominatrices. Here Yva Richard. 1920s. Collection Alexandre Dupouy, author of *Yva Richard - L'âge d'or du fétichisme*. 1994

Photos by Roger Schall for the girlie magazine *Pour Lire à Deux*. 1936.
▶▶ The vamp *par excellence* in the 1930s, Marlene, in *The Blue Angel* · Der Supervamp der 30er Jahre, Marlene
Dietrich, in „Der Blaue Engel" · La super-vamp des années 30, Marlene, dans « L'Ange bleu » **68 · 69**

The provocative *suspender belt* mark one: Liza Minnelli recreates 1930s Berlin in Bob Fosse's *Cabaret* · *Strapse,* die verrückt machen... Erste Version: Liza Minnelli erfindet das Berlin der 30er Jahre neu. Szenen aus dem Film „Cabaret" von Bob Fosse · Le *porte-jarretelles* qui rend fou... 1re version: Liza Minnelli réinvente le Berlin des années 30, dans «Cabaret», de Bob Fosse. 1972

◄ The provocative *suspender belt* mark two: Hanna Schygulla in *The Marriage of Maria Braun* by R. W. Fassbinder · *Strapse, die verrückt machen...* Zweite Version: Hanna Schygulla in „Die Ehe der Maria Braun" von R. W. Fassbinder · Le *porte-jarretelles qui rend fou...* 2e version : Hanna Schygulla, dans « Le Mariage de Maria Braun », de R. W. Fassbinder. 1978

► And its sequel, mark three: Barbara Sukowa, in *Lola*, also by R. W. Fassbinder · Dritte Version: Barbara Sukowa in „Lola" von R. W. Fassbinder · Et sa suite, 4e version : Barbara Sukowa, dans « Lola », du même R. W. Fassbinder. 1981
►► From the musical *Too Much Harmony*. 1933

R.W. Fassbinder

Où
se termine
**LE MARIAGE DE
MARIA BRAUN**
commence...

Lola

UNE FEMME ALLEMANDE

Rainer Werner Fassbinder .... Barbara Sukowa / Mario Adorf / Armin Mueller-Stahl

1452-114

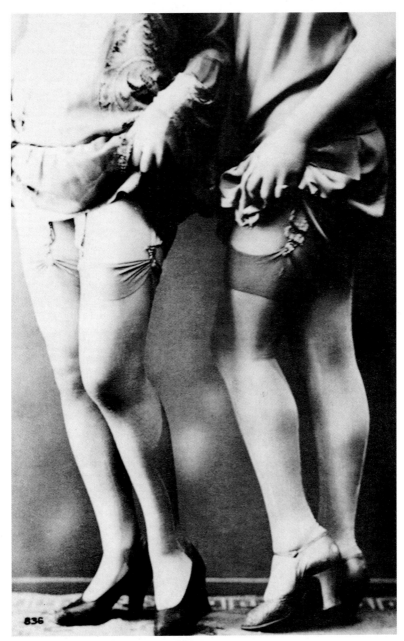

◄ Laure Albin-Guillot: *Stockings* series. A woman photographing the feminine appeal of lingerie · Serie über die *Strümpfe*. Eine Frau fotografiert die Weiblichkeit der Dessous… · Laure Albin Guillot: Série sur les *bas*. Une femme photographie la féminité des dessous… 1930s

PHOTO LAURE ALBIN GUILLOT

Le soutien gorge

Cibil

BREVETÉ S. G. D. G.

tient et maintient
sans épaulettes

The Cibil strapless *bra* · Der *Büstenhalter* „Cibil", der ohne Träger hält · Le *soutien-gorge* «Cibil», qui tient tout seul sans épaulettes. Photographed by Laure Albin Guillot. 1930s.

▲ Sadomasochistic outfit made of metal · SM-Garnitur aus Metall · Ensemble métallique sado-maso. 1933
►► A woman's complete outfit 1925–1930: bobbed hair, *chemise,* wide *suspenders* and *stockings,* shoes with straps · Die komplette Ausrüstung der Frau 1925–1930: kurz geschnittene Haare, Hemdröckchen, breite Strumpfhalter, Strümpfe und Schuhe mit Fesselriemen · Le harnachement complet de la femme 1925–1930 : cheveux courts, chemise, larges jarretelles et bas, souliers à brides.

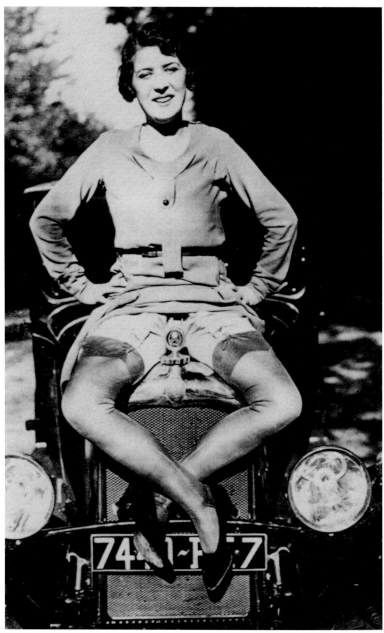

The modern woman coming to grips with a new rival, the motor car · Die moderne Frau im Wett-streit mit einer neuen Rivalin, der Limousine · La femme moderne aux prises avec une nouvelle rivale, l'automobile. C. 1927

▼ Drawing by Giffey: *The Breakdown · Die Panne · La Panne.* 1930s

In France, paid holidays were demanted by law in 1927. Freed from work, women treating all and sundry to a view of the underwear and *suspenders* beneath their flimsy dresses. Postcards from the time · Urlaubszeit 1927. Auch die Frauen nützen diese Tage und zeigen freizügig ihre Dessous und Strumpfhalter unter ihren leichten Sommerklei-

dern. Postkarten aus jener Epoche · 1927, ce sont les congés payés. La femme montrant librement ses dessous et ses jarretelles sous des robes légères. Cartes postales de l'époque.

Platinum blonde: Jean Harlow, the new vamp of the 1930s · Die platinblonde Jean Harlow, der neue Vamp der 30er Jahre · La « blonde platinée », Jean Harlow, nouvelle Vamp des années 30.

The underwear worn by beautiful Southerners during the American Civil War: Vivien Leigh in *Gone with the Wind* by Victor Fleming · Auch die schönen Südstaatlerinnen aus der Zeit des Sezessionskrieges zeigen sich gern in Dessous, zumindest im Film, wie hier Vivien Leigh. Szene aus dem Film „Vom Winde verweht" von Victor Fleming · Les dessous des belles Sudistes pendant la guerre de Sécession, ou Vivien Leigh , dans « Autant en emporte le vent », de Victor Fleming. 1939

▲ Manassé: The vamp's underwear in a post-cubist setting, Hungary · Die Dessous eines Vamps in einem postku-
bistischen Dekor, Ungarn · Les dessous de la Vamp dans un décor post-cubiste, Hongrie. C. 1930–1935
◄ Arletty, in *camiknickers*, has her hand kissed by Dalio in *Tempête* by Bernard-Deschamps · Arletty im Hemd-
höschen, Dalio küßt ihr die Hand. Szene aus „Tempête" von Bernard-Deschamps · Arletty, en *combinaison-
culotte*, et le baise-main de Dalio, dans « Tempête », de Bernard-Deschamps. 1939

Manassé: The vamp's underwear, Hungary · Die Dessous eines Vamps, Ungarn · Manassé: Les dessous de la Vamp, Hongrie. C. 1930–1935

►► Everything you ever wanted to know about the life of a French maid · Das Leben der Soubretten ist wie ein offenes Buch... · On n'ignore rien de la vie des soubrettes...

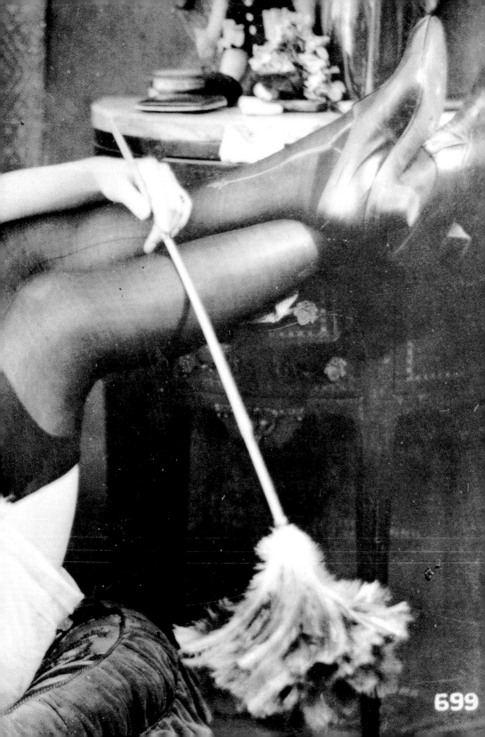

699

BY REDFERN

▲ Warner used skiing, a luxury sport at the time, to promote its elasticised range of lingerie · Um die Elastizität seiner Modelle anzupreisen, bedient sich auch „Warner" des Skisports, zu jener Zeit ein Luxus · « Warner » utilise aussi le ski, sport de luxe à l'époque, pour vanter l'élasticité de ses modèles. 1937
▶ Le Gant, made of "youthlastic", so stretchy it fitted like a glove, was perfect for women at the wheel · „Le Gant" aus „Youthlastic", der sich dehnt wie ein Handschuh, eignet sich bestens für die Frau am Steuer · « Le Gant », en « youthlastic », qui s'étire comme un gant, convient à la femme au volant. 1935

Jacques Henri Lartigue: *Woman Skiing · Skiläuferin · Skieuse*. 1940s

Kurt Hutton: *Two at the Fair* · *Die Zwei auf dem Jahrmarkt* · *Two at the Fair*. London. 1938

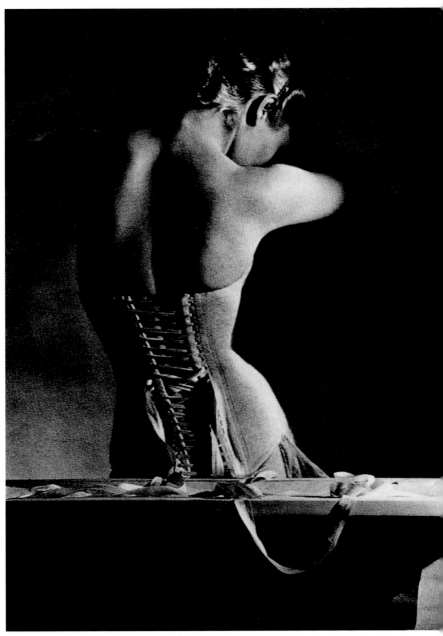

Horst P. Horst: *Corset* for *Vogue* · *Korsett*, für „Vogue" · *Corset*, pour « Vogue ». 1939

eter Driben: Cover of *Silk Stockings* · Titelblatt zu „Silk Stocking" · Couverture de « Silk Stocking » (« Bas de Soie ») 1938

Marcel Rochas invented the *waspie* · Marcel Rochas erfindet die *Guêpière* · Marcel Rochas invente la *guêpière*. 1945

The New Look *waspie*, France
Die *Guêpière* zum „New Look", Frankreich
La *guêpière* du « New Look », France. 1947

The art of striptease, which draws its origins from 19th-century acts like the *Coucher d'Yvette* in Paris, a great favourite with Toulouse-Lautrec and his friends, reached its apogee in the United States. It then crossed back over the Atlantic and set up strip joints in all the capitals of Europe. Here, the famous Crazy Horse in Paris, shortly after it opened. 1950s

Die Bezeichnung Striptease kommt zwar aus Amerika, entstanden ist er aber im vergangenen Jahrhundert in Paris mit den ersten Entblätterungen im Stil „Coucher d'Yvette", die schon Toulouse-Lautrec und seine Freunde so begeisterten. Aus Amerika ist er dann wieder über den Atlantik zurückgekommen und hat in sämtlichen europäischen Hauptstädten seine Tempel errichtet. Hier das berühmte „Crazy Horse" in seinen Anfängen. Paris. 50er Jahre

Né à Paris, au siècle dernier, avec les premiers effeuillages de type « Coucher d'Yvette » qu'affectionnaient Toulouse-Lautrec et ses amis, le strip-tease a trouvé son nom, et conquis ses galons, aux Etats-Unis. Puis il a franchi l'Atlantique dans l'autre sens et a installé ses temples dans toutes les capitales européennes. Ici, le célèbre « Crazy Horse » à ses débuts, Paris. Années 50

Jennie Lee

Besides her duly-recorded claim to having the biggest bust in burlesque—a phenomenal 42 inches—she also performs remarkable maneuvers with well-placed tassles.

In the 1950s, Jennie Lee, a burlesque star of the time, was a huge success twirling her tassels every which way · In den 50er Jahren war Jennie Lee, Star der erotischen Burleske höchst erfolgreich mit ihrer Nummer, die Troddeln an ihren Brüsten in alle Richtungen kreisen zu lassen · Dans les années 50, Jennie Lee remporte un grand succès en faisant tourner ses pompons dans tous les sens...

uring the same period, in America, striptease became more democratic. To rekindle their husbands' ardour, wives
uld go to special schools to learn how to strip, using provocative lingerie like true professionals. Here, a teacher shows
em the ropes · Zur selben Zeit wird der Striptease in Amerika demokratisiert. Um ihren Ehemännern mehr Appetit zu
achen, lernen die Ehefrauen in speziellen Schulen, sich mit Hilfe verführerischer Dessous professionell zu enthüllen.
er gibt die Lehrerin ein Beispiel · A la même époque, le strip-tease se démocratise en Amérique. Pour réveiller les
deurs de leurs maris, les épouses apprennent, dans des écoles spécialisées, à s'effeuiller à grand renfort de dessous sug-
stifs, comme de vraies professionnelles. Ici, un professeur montrant l'exemple... 1950s

▲ Elsa Martinelli in *The Rice Field* by Raffaello Matarazzo · Elsa Martinelli in „Das Reismädchen" von Raffaello Mata-
razzo · Elsa Martinelli, dans «La Rizière», de Raffaello Matarazzo. 1956
▶ Silvana Mangano in *Bitter Rice* by Giuseppe De Santis · Silvana Mangano in „Bitterer Reis" von Giuseppe De Santis
· Silvana Mangano, dans «Riz amer», de Giuseppe De Santis. 1949

Lesage for Scandale. As in Walt Disney's animated cartoon film, enchanting little birds are weaving stockings for Cinderella · Lesage für „Scandale". Wie in dem Zeichentrickfilm „Aschenputtel" von Walt Disney umgarnen reizende Vögel die *Strümpfe* der vom Himmel gefallenen Schönen... · Lesage, pour « Scandale ». Comme dans le dessin animé « Cendrillon », de Walt Disney, de charmants oiseaux tissent les *bas* de cette beauté tombée du ciel... C. 1950

le bas de qualité

BEL

Anonymous for Bel *stockings*. Yet more birds, but these are doves, symbols of gentleness, femininity and Venus ·
Anonym: Werbung für die *Strümpfe* „Bel". Auch hier fliegen Vögel herum, diesmal sind es Tauben – sie stehen für
Sanftheit und Weiblichkeit... · Anonyme, pour le *bas* «Bel». Les oiseaux sont encore là, ce sont des colombes, sym-
boles de douceur et de féminité... 1951

elle maintient !

Les sports, la voiture, les affaires, imposent aux femmes des fatigues qu'ignoraient leurs grand' mères. La gaine SCANDALE sait compenser les faiblesses du corps féminin et cependant lui laisser toute sa souplesse et son aisance.

Beauté et santé sont l'œuvre de la gaine SCANDALE. *Son tulle garanti* au tissage spécialement étudié, fait que souple et ferme tout à la fois elle moule sans causer aucune gêne. Et la coquetterie n'y perd pas ses droits. La ligne actuelle de la mode ne tolérant aucune imperfection, la gaine SCANDALE invisible et toujours présente, modélera votre corps aux mesures exactes qu'imposent nos couturiers.

SCANDALE

PARIS : 26, Rue Vignon ; 73, Faubourg Saint-Honoré ; 36 bis, Avenue de l'Opéra ; 17, Boulevard Raspail LYON : 7, Rue de la République. — MARSEILLE : 11, Rue de la Darse. — NICE : 1, Rue du Maréchal Pétain. BRUXELLES : 101, Rue de Namur. — LONDRES : 81, Great Portland Street. — TURIN : 237, Corso Vitto Emanuele II. — BEYROUTH, Souk Tawile. CHEZ LES BONNES CORSETIÈRES ET DANS LES GRANDS MAGASI

LA GAINE EN TULLE GARANTI

NUE OU NON non bien sûr, mais presque oui

Ste des MATIÈRES PLASTIQUES
M. R. B.
7, Boulevard Pasteur, 7
93 - LA COURNEUVE
TÉLÉPH. 833-98-99
54 N 7320

Découvrir COMBINU de Barbara,
c'est parfaire votre ligne
en ayant l'impression d'être presque nue.
C'est être silhouettée sans aucune gêne.
C'est concilier l'inconciliable
avec la nouvelle texture extra-fine de Barbara.
Elle vous offre huit façons d'être nue ou non,
en uni, en florisé, en blanc, en chair.

16, faubourg saint-denis - Paris 10ᵉ - téléphone 824.53.99

combinu
pantynu
de
Barbara

▲ With Barbara, woman were almost naked · Mit „Barbara" ist die Frau so gut wie nackt · Avec « Barbara », la femme est presque nue. 1960s
◄ With Scandale, they could run and jump · Mit „Scandale" darf sie sogar Luftsprünge machen · Avec « Scandale », elle a le droit de sauter en l'air. Late 1950s

◄ Marilyn wearing *fishnet tights* or black *stockings,* posing, shortly before her death, for her friend, the photographer Milton Greene · Marilyn in *Netzstrumpfhose* und in *schwarzen Strümpfen,* kurz vor ihrem Tod fotografiert von ihrem Freund Milton Greene · Marilyn en *collant-résille,* ou en *bas noirs,* posant, peu de temps avant sa mort, pour le photographe Milton Greene.

According to legend, the only time Marilyn Monroe ever wore knickers was for Billy Wilder's *The Seven Year Itch* · Böse Zungen behaupten, Marilyn Monroe habe nur ein einziges Mal in ihrem Leben Unterhöschen getragen, nämlich für den Film „Das verflixte siebte Jahr" von Billy Wilder · D'après les mauvaises langues, la seule fois de sa vie où Marilyn Monroe porta une *culotte* : pour les besoins de « Sept Ans de réflexion », de Billy Wilder. 1955

▲At the Cannes Festival in 1956, the already famous Bardot showed her *briefs* to the press photographers · 1956 gewährt die inzwischen berühmte B. B. bei den Filmfestspielen in Cannes den Pressefotografen einen Blick unter ihre Röcke... · L'année 1956, au Festival de Cannes, la déjà célèbre B. B. n'hésite pasà montrer sa petite *culotte* aux photographes de presse...

▶Bardot, still beautiful at the age of 40, photographed by Ghislain Dussart, for the shooting of *Viva Maria* by Louis Malle · B. B., schön wie immer, fotografiert von Ghislain Dussart während der Dreharbeiten zu „Viva Maria" von Louis Malle · B. B., toujours belle, photographiée par Ghislain Dussart, lors du tournage de « Viva Maria », de Louis Malle. 1965

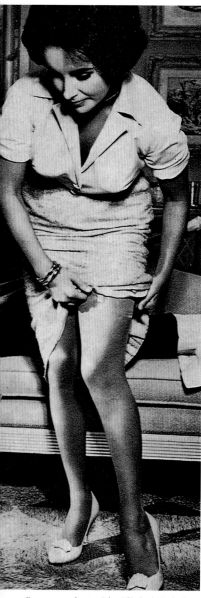

From *suspenders* to *tights:* Elizabeth Taylor's underwear on screen in *Cat on a Hot Tin Roof* by Richard Brooks, 1958, and off · Die Palette der Dessous von Elizabeth Taylor im Film reicht von *Strapsen* bis zur *Strumpfhose.* Szene aus „Die Katze auf dem heißen Blechdach" von Richard Brooks. Die Taylor privat... · Des *jarretelles* au *collant,* ou les dessous d'Elizabeth Taylor au cinéma, dans « La Chatte sur un toit brûlant », de Richard Brooks. 1958. Et dans le privé...

A cult film gave its name to an item of lingerie and boosted sales of these nightdresses to the tune of twenty-five million: Carroll Baker in *Baby Doll*, by Elia Kazan · Ein Kultfilm gab einem Wäschestück seinen Namen und bewirkte, daß davon mehr als 25 Millionen Stück verkauft wurden: Carroll Baker in „Baby Doll" von Elia Kazan · Le cas où un film-culte donna son nom à une pièce de lingerie et en fit vendre plus de vingt-cinq millions d'exemplaires : « Baby Doll », d'Elia Kazan. Carroll Baker, en *nuisette,* ne fit pas seulement vendre son « Baby Doll ». 1956

The striptease according to Fellini: Nadia Gray in *La dolce vita* · Ein Striptease à la Fellini: Nadia Gray in „La Dolce Vita".
Le strip-tease selon Fellini: Nadia Gray, dans « La Dolce Vita ». 1959

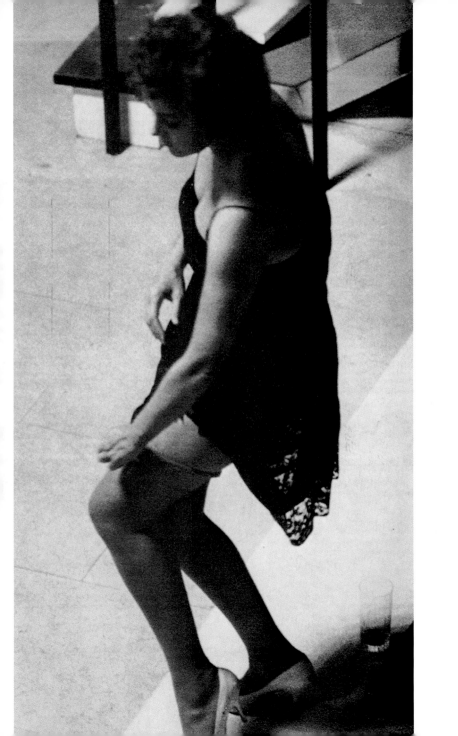

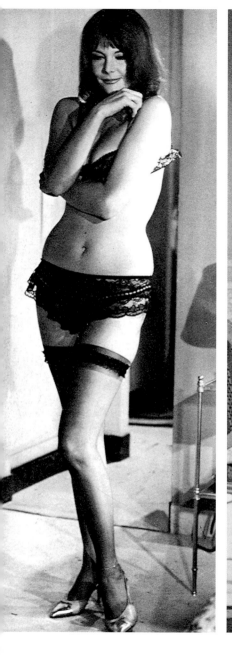

A classic example of the art of striptease on screen: Françoise Brion in *La Dénonciation* by Jacques Doniol-Valcroze · Ein klassischer Striptease im Film: Françoise Brion in „La Dénonciation" von Jacques Doniol-Valcroze · Un classique de l'effeuillage au cinéma : Françoise Brion, dans « La Dénonciation », de Jacques Doniol-Valcroze. 1961

►► Not forgetting the famous striptease by Raquel Welch, who removes her *knickers* in front of an audience including John Huston · Dieser berühmte Striptease von Raquel Welch bleibt unvergessen – vor den Augen von John Huston läßt sie ihren Slip fallen · *Sans oublier le fameux strip-tease de Raquel Welch, qui en perd sa culotte sous les yeux de John Huston spectateur... 1960s

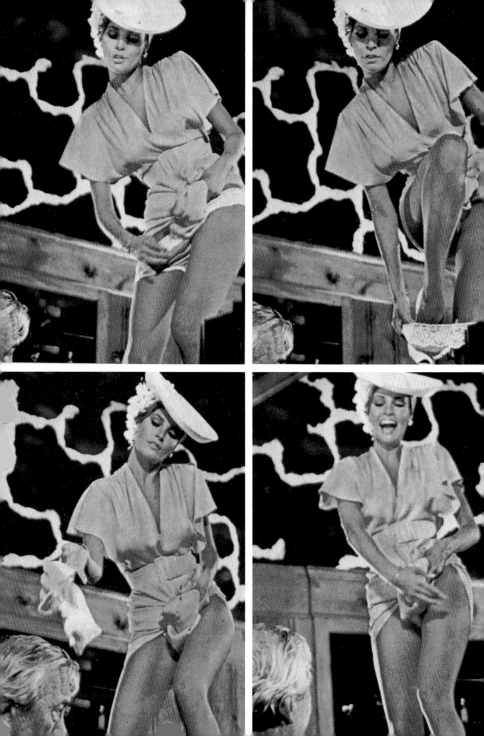

The curvaceous Elsa Martinelli, the star of *And to Die of Pleasure, The Threat* and *Misdeal,* stripping down to her black *stockings* for the last time, at the age of 46, in front of the photographer's camera

Die attraktive Elsa Martinelli, Star der Filme „Und vor Lust zu sterben", „Die Drohung" und „Maldonne", enthüllt sich anläßlich ihres 46. Geburtstags zum letzten Mal vor dem Objektiv des Fotografen.

La pulpeuse Elsa Martinelli, vedette de « Et mourir de plaisir », « La Menace » et « Maldonne » effeuillant une dernière fois ses dessous noirs, à l'occasion de ses 46 ans, devant l'objectif du photographe...

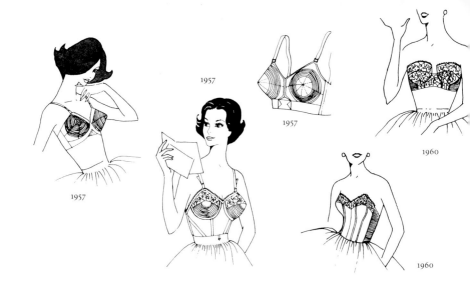

1957

1957

1957

1960

1960

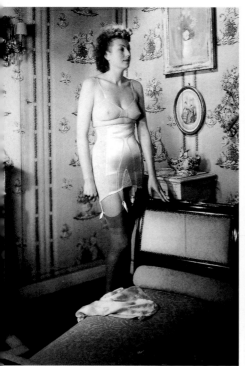

▲ Line drawings by Jean Weber for *Fashion in Underwear* · Zeichnungen von Jean Weber für „Fashion in Underwear" · Dessins de Jean Weber pour « Fashion in Underwear ». 1971

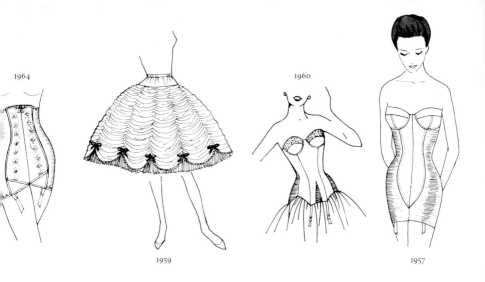

1964

1959

1960

1957

▼ Four Oriano designs · Vier Modelle „Oriano" · Quatre modèles « Oriano ». 1950–1951

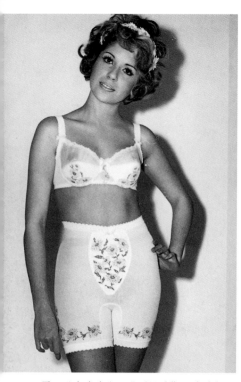

▲ Three Aubade designs · Drei Modelle „Aubade" · Trois modèles « Aubade ». 1951–1952

1970

1960

1961

1963

▼ Line drawings by Jean Weber for *Fashion in Underwear* · Zeichnungen von Jean Weber für „Fashion in Underwear" · Dessins de Jean Weber pour «Fashion in Underwear». 1971

1958

1967

1967

◄► *Hold-ups.* Germany · *Halterlose Strümpfe,*
Deutschland. · *Bas autocollants,*
Allemagne. 1960s

▲ Le Bourget *hold-ups* and matching lingerie made of
stretch Lycra lace, France · *Halterlose Strümpfe und
Zweiteiler* aus passender Lycra-Spitze „Le Bourget",
Frankreich · *Bas autocollants et deux pièces* en dentelle
Lycra assortie « Le Bourget », France. 1960s

Laura Antonelli
& Claudia
Cardinale

Prostitute by day and a respectable woman by night, Catherine Deneuve at the brothel, in *Belle de Jour* by Luis Buñuel · Catherine Deneuve, Prostituierte am Tage und ehrbare Bürgerin in der übrigen Zeit, in „Belle de Jour – Schöne des Tages" von Luis Buñuel · Prostituée le jour et bourgeoise le reste du temps, Catherine Deneuve « en maison », dans « Belle de Jour », de Luis Buñuel. 1967

Ursula Andress changes her style of underwear from film to film · Auch
Ursula Andress zeigt in jedem Film neue Dessous · De film en film, Ursula
Andress change de dessous... 1960s

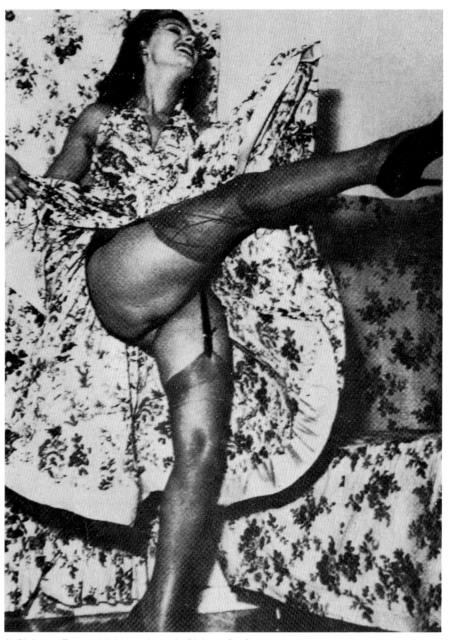

Sophia Loren off screen · Die Loren privat... · Sophia Loren dans le privé...
► Sophia Loren's consummate striptease in *Yesterday, Today and Tomorrow* by Vittorio de Sica · Ein grandioser Strip-

tease: Sophia Loren in „Gestern, Heute, Morgen" von Vittorio De Sica · Un chef-d'œuvre de strip-tease, celui de Sophia Loren, dans « Hier, aujourd'hui, demain », de Vittorio de Sica. 1963.

In 1967, Arthur Penn's film *Bonnie and Clyde* was a great hit. Jean Feldman immediately capitalised on this, depicting his "Bonnies" in Ergé *hold-ups,* extremely practical for – well – hold-ups · 1967 hat Arthur Penns Film „Bonnie and Clyde" sensationellen Erfolg. Jean Feldman nutzt ihn sofort für seine Zwecke und zeigt seine „Bon-

nies" in halterlosen Strümpfen von „Ergé", die sich für einen Bankraub bestens eignen · En 1967, le film d'Arthur
Penn, « Bonnie and Clyde », remporte un triomphe. Jean Feldman s'en empare aussitôt et montre ses « Bonnies »,
équipées de *bas* « Ergé » autocollants, bien pratiques pour attaquer les banques...

▲ A veiled reference to the good old *corset*, with this *tights-and-corset* one-piece · Mit einem Augenzwinkern: Die Strumpfhose mit integriertem Korsett · Un clin d'œil au bon vieux *corset*, avec le *collant* à *corset* incorporé. 1967
◄ Jeanloup Sieff: *New York*. 1962

A dazzling array of *panty girdles*. From left to right: Kaiser: *panty girdle* and matching *bra*. 1960s–70s. Aubade: style of *panty girdle* and *bra*. 1960s–70s. Model in her *panty girdle* waiting her turn in the catwalk parade. In *Vogue*. 1970s

Reigen der *Panties*. Von links nach rechts: „Kaiser", *Panty und BH*, zusammenpassend. 60er bis 70er Jahre. „Aubade", Modell eines *Panty* und *Büstenhalters*. 60er bis 70er Jahre. Mannequin im *Panty* wartet beim Défilé auf ihren Auftritt, in „Vogue". 70er Jahre

La ronde des *panties*. De gauche à droite: «Kaiser», *panty et soutien-gorge* assorti. Années 60-70, «Aubade», modèle de *panty* et *soutien-gorge*. Années 60-70. Mannequin en *panty* attendant le défilé, dans «Vogue». Années 70

In the 1960s–70s, loose-fitting underwear again carried the day. Line drawings by Jean Weber for *Fashion in Underwear*. 1971

In den 60er und 70er Jahren gewinnt wieder das Weichfließende die Oberhand. Zeichnungen von Jean Weber für „Fashion in Underwear". 1971

Dans les années 60–70, une fois de plus, le «souple» finit par l'emporter. Dessins de Jean Weber pour «Fashion in Underwear». 1971

Women now seemed to have turned their back on restrictive undergarments. Lingerie show in 1970 · Die Einschnü-
rung früherer Zeiten hat die Frau offensichtlich abgelegt. Wäschepräsentation von 1970 · La Femme cependant,
semble avoir rejeté les anciens carcans. Présentation de lingerie en 1970.

Knickers for sportswomen · Das Höschen zum Tennisdress · La petite *culotte* des sportives. Wimbledon. 1960s

In, "Hot Lips", the desirable major portrayed by Sally Kellerman, gets out of her helicopter, treating the troops to a generous glimpse of her *suspenders*. *M.A.S.H.* by Robert Altman · Der attraktive Major Sally Kellermann steigt aus dem Hubschrauber und läßt die Soldaten offenherzig ihre *Strapse* sehen. „M.A.S.H." von Robert Altman · La ravissante major, dite «lèvres en feu», Sally Kellerman, débarque de son hélicoptère en montrant généreusement aux troupes son *porte-jarretelles...* «M.A.S.H.», de Robert Altman. 1970

The society prostitute: Monica Vitti in *Histoire d'aimer* by Marcello Fondato · Die mondäne Prostituierte: Monica Vitti in „Histoire d'aimer" von Marcello Fondato · La prostituée mondaine: Monica Vitti, dans «Histoire d'aimer», de Marcello Fondato. 1970s

The lingerie worn by Romy Schneider in *Orage* · Romy Schneiders Wäsche in „Orage" · La lingerie de Romy Schneider, dans « Orage ». 1970s

▲ Triumph, Warner and Scandale designs are shown alongside cigar bands or beer labels · Modelle von „Triumph", „Warner" und „Scandale" in Verbindung mit Bauchbinden von Zigarren und Bieretiketten · Présentation des modèles « Triumph », « Warner » et « Scandale », en relation avec des bagues de cigares ou des bières... Photos by Helmut Newton. 1970

▶ Dim. Narcissism of the model, voyeurism of the spectator · „Dim". Hier werden Wünsche wahr: die Selbstverliebte im Blick des Voyeurs… · « Dim ». Narcissisme du modèle et voyeurisme du spectateur. 1971

▲ *Panty girdles* made of Lycra, 9 colours, Printemps department store, Paris · *Panties* aus Lycra, neun Farbtöne, Magasins du Printemps, Paris · *Panties* en lycra, 9 coloris, magasins du Printemps, Paris. 1967
◄ Mary Quant, inventor of the miniskirt: Embroidered *tights* · Mary Quant, die Erfinderin des Minirocks, präsentiert eine bestickte Strumpfhose · Mary Quant, inventeur de la minijupe, *collant* brodé. 1965

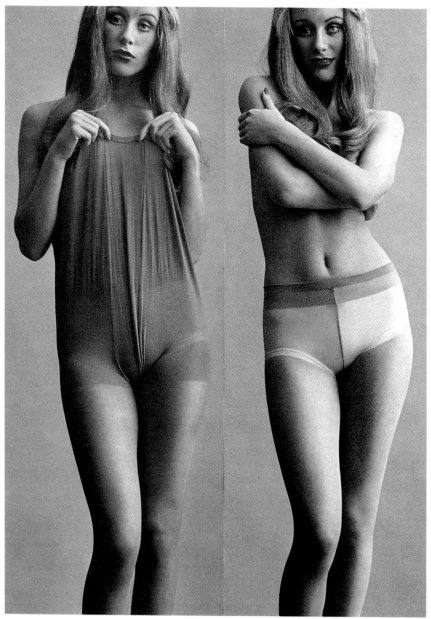

▲ Pretty Polly, stretch Lycra *tights* · „Pretty Polly", elastische *Strumpfhose* aus Lycra · « Pretty Polly », *collant* extensible en Lycra. 1972

► Jeanloup Sieff: Publicity photo for Youpee *tights* from Dim · Werbefoto für die Strumpfhose „Youpee" von „Dim".
Photo publicitaire pour le *collant* « Youpee » de « Dim ». 1972

▲ Dim *tights* in 8 colours. 1971–1972 collection · Strumpfhosen „Dim", acht Farbtöne. Kollektion 1971–1972 · *Collants* «Dim», en 8 coloris. Collection 1971–1972

◄ Embroidered *tights* by Chantal Thomass. · Bestickte Strumpfhose „Chantal Thomass". · *Collant* brodé «Chantal Thomass». 1970

▲ Sequence from *Malicia* by Salvatore Samberi. This lascivious comedy was a huge success in Italy · Szene aus „Malizia" von Salvatore Samberi. Diese freizügige Komödie löste in Italien Entsetzen aus · Séquence de « Malicia » de Salvatore Samberi. Cette comédie salace fit un malheur en Italie. 1973

◄ Another way of revealing your underwear to a young companion. Susan Player in *L'Initiatrice* by Sergio Martino · Auch eine Art, einem jungen Freund seine Dessous vorzuführen. Susan Player in „L'Initiatrice" von Sergio Martino · Autre façon de dévoiler ses dessous à un jeune camarade. Susan Player, dans « L'Initiatrice », de Sergio Martino. 1970s

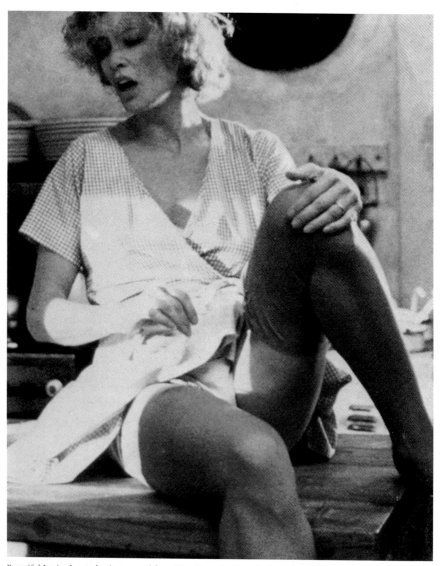

Beautiful Jessica Lange, having escaped from King-Kong, is now seducing Jack Nicholson on the kitchen table in *The Postman Always Rings Twice* · Die schöne Jessica Lange, kaum den Klauen King Kongs entronnen, verführt nun Jack Nicholson auf ihrem Küchentisch in „Wenn der Postmann zweimal klingelt" von Bob Rafelson · La belle Jessica Lange, qui a échappé à King-Kong, séduit maintenant Jack Nicholson sur la table de sa cuisine, dans « Le Facteur sonne toujours deux fois », de Bob Rafelson. 1980

▶ Jack Nicholson pulling off Jessica Lange's *knickers*. Censored sequence · Jack Nicholson zieht Jessica Lange das Höschen aus. Zensierte Szene · Jack Nicholson arrachant la *culotte* de Jessica Lange. Séquence censurée

►► In *The Key* by Tinto Brass, the elderly husband with a fetish for underwear takes advantage of his wife's accommodating sleep to photograph and rape her · In „Der Schlüssel" von Tinto Brass, nutzt der alternde Ehemann, ein Wäschefetischist, den vorgetäuschten Schlaf seiner Gattin, um sie zu fotografieren und zu vergewaltigen · Dans « La Clé », de Tinto Brass, le vieux mari, fétichiste des dessous, profite du sommeil complice de son épouse, pour la photographier et la violer... 1984

LA CLÉ

Interdit aux moins de 18 ans   ugc   V de C 10414

Nastassja Kinski girds her loins in *Maria's Lovers* · Nastassja Kinski macht sich in „Maria's Lovers" zum Angriff bereit · Nastassja Kinski affûte ses armes, dans « Maria's Lovers ». 1984

It took no less than six films and as many directors to recount the erotic escapades of *Emmanuelle*. In the first, made in 1973 by Just Jaeckin, Sylvia Kristel plays the heroine · Nicht weniger als sechs Filme und ebenso viele Regisseure erzählen die erotischen Abenteuer von „Emmanuelle". Im ersten von 1973 (Regie: Just Jaeckin) spielt Sylvia Kristel die Titelrolle · Pas moins de six films et autant de réalisateurs, pour conter les aventures érotiques d'«Emmanuelle». Dans le premier, réalisé en 1973 de Just Jaeckin, Sylvia Kristel, joue l'héroïne.

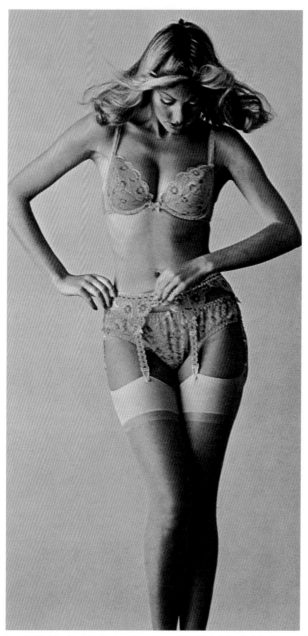

The Natural Look, launched in New York in the 80s · Der „Natural Look", in New York in den 8oer Jahren
kreiert · Le « Natural Look », lancé à New York dans les années 80
◄Gemma lingerie set · Modell „Gemma" · Modèle « Gemma ». 1985

▲ In the 1990s, knickers became extremely brief, almost non-existent · In den 90er Jahren werden die *Slips* immer unsichtbarer, sie verschwinden sozusagen · Dans les années 90, les *slips* deviennent évanescents, quasi inexistants ► Gossard sheer underwear. *Bra, bodysuit* and *briefs* have become invisible · „Gossard" mit seinen Dessous „Die zweite Haut". *BH, Body, Slip* sind unsichtbar geworden · «Gossard» et ses dessous «seconde peau». *Soutien-gorge, body, slip* sont devenus invisibles.

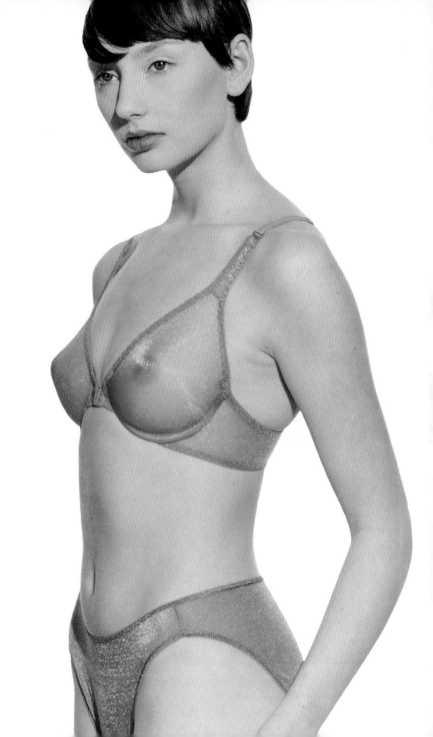

Luxury packaging for bottoms: feminine but a little kinky with provocative cut-outs. Also deceptive packaging, using padding to swell the truth · Luxusverpackungen für den Po, ein wenig geschummelt und ein wenig pervers mit

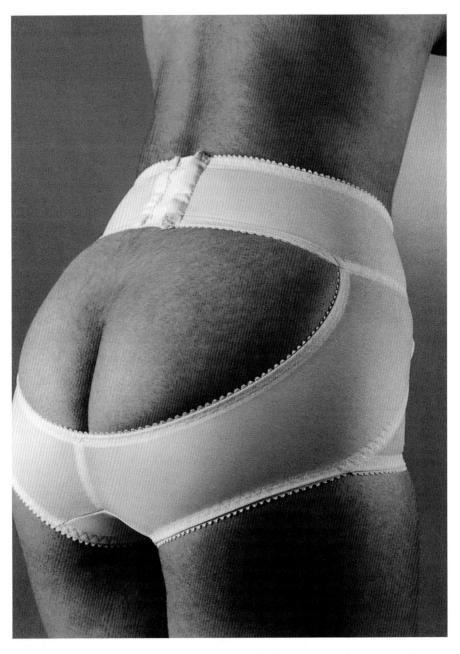

verführerischem Ausschnitt · Emballages de luxe pour « derrières » féminins, mais un peu plus pervers, avec découpe suggestive. Emballages tricheurs aussi, avec rembourrages qui mentent... « Bella », Turin. 1997   **172 · 173**

Artistic *tights* draw their inspiration from the last century. Drawings by Aubrey Beardsley. 1896. Photos by Eric Kroll. 1996 · Die gemusterte Strumpfhose ist beeinflußt von Motiven des vergangenen Jahrhunderts. Zeichnungen von Aubrey Beardsley. 1896. Fotos von Eric Kroll. 1996

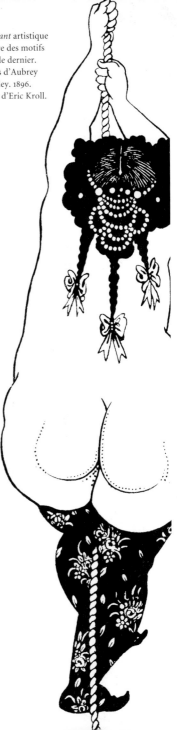

Le *Collant* artistique s'inspire des motifs du siècle dernier. Dessins d'Aubrey Beardsley. 1896. Photos d'Eric Kroll. 1996

From left to right: *Fishnet tights,* leopard-skin print, *suspender belt style tights,* a compromise between the two, *lace suspender belt* and, the height of fetishism, *suspender belt* with matching *garter!* · Von links nach rechts: Netzstrumpf-hose, Leopardenmuster, Hüftgürtel-Strumpfhose, Kombination aus den beiden; Strapse aus Spitze und, als Krönung

des Fetischismus, Strapse mit passendem Strumpfband! · De gauche à droite : *Collant filet résille*, impression léopard, *collant-porte-jarretelles* compromis entre les deux, *porte-jarretelles* en dentelle et, le comble du fétichisme, *porte-jarretelles* avec *jarretière* assortie ! 1997

Eric Kroll: *Tights* and high-heeled shoes for masochistic fetishists · *Strumpfhose* und hochhackige Schuhe für Maso-Fetischisten... · *Collant* et chaussures haut perchées pour fétichistes maso... 1996

Eric Kroll: The modern woman with the added phantasm of an Indian squaw disguise · Die moderne Frau, als Squaw verkleidet · La femme moderne avec le fantasme en prime de la fausse squaw indienne. 1994

BRIGITTE NIELSEN

▲ Eric Kroll: The confident, assertive modern woman · Die moderne Frau, selbstsicher und beherschend · La femme moderne, sûre d'elle et dominatrice. 1994
◄ Draped with chains that are more protective than aggressive, Brigitte Nielsen, former Mrs Rambo, embodies the type of assertive woman · Brigitte Nielsen, Exfreundin von „Rambo", mit Ketten geschmückt, die ebenso schützend wie aggressiv wirken, ist die Inkarnation der starken Frau · Bardée de chaînes protectrices autant qu'agressives, Brigitte Nielsen, ex-Madame « Rambo », incarne la femme dominatrice. 1997

▲ Velda Lauder, London. Photo Robert Chouraqui. 1995
► Paco Rabanne: *Underwear-outerwear,* made of soft ostrich leather · „Paco Rabanne“: *Dessous-dessus* aus Straußen-
leder · « Paco Rabanne », *Dessous-dessus,* en cuir d'autruche. 1993

paco ra

Madonna enjoys shocking her audience by showing off her futuristic *corset*, with its pointed breasts shaped like live shells, designed for her by Jean-Paul Gaultier, and by throwing her *knickers* into the crowd... · Madonna liebt es ihr Publikum zu schockieren, sei es durch Auftritte im futuristischen *Korsett* mit granatenförmigen Brüsten, das Jean-Paul Gaultier für sie entworfen hat, oder indem sie ihr *Höschen* in die Menge wirft... Madonna aime choquer son public en exhibant le *corset* futuriste, aux seins en form d'obus, créé pour elle par Jean-Paul Gaultier, et en jetant sa *culotte* dans la foule... 1995

Pure, London: Matching vinyl *corset, knickers, suspenders* and boots · „Pure", London: *Korsett, Slip, Strumpfhalter* und passende Stiefel aus Vinyl · «Pure», Londres: *Corset, slip, jarretelles* et bottes coordonnés en vinyl.
▶ From *Inside-Out*, the lingerie of the 1990s shows SM tendencies. Demask, Amsterdam. Vinyl *corset* · Mit dem „Des

sous-dessus" tendiert die Reizwäsche der 90er Jahre zum SM-Outfit. „Demask", Amsterdam, Korsett aus Vinyl · De
« dessous-dessus », la lingerie des années 90 tend vers le SM (sadomasochisme). « Demask », Amsterdam, *corset* en
vinyl. Photos Robert Chouraqui. 1996   **186 · 187**

Designs by Michel Coulon that would not look out of place at the Georges Pompidou Centre in Paris · Kreationen „Michel Coulon", die eine Zierde für das Centre Pompidou wären... · Des créations « Michel Coulon », qui ne

déspareraient pas le Centre Pompidou... Photos Robert Chouraqui. 1996

"Michel Coulon" designs · Kreationen „Michel Coulon" · Créations « Michel Coulon ». Photo Robert Chouraqui. 1996

Copyright · Bildnachweis · Credits photographiques

Unless otherwise specified, copyright on the works reproduced lies with the respective photographers. Despite intensive research it has not always been possible to establish copyright ownership. Where this is the case we would appreciate notification.

Das Copyright für die abgebildeten Werke liegt, sofern nicht nachfolgend anders aufgeführt, bei den jeweiligen Fotografen und Künstlern. Trotz intensiver Recherche konnten die Urheberrechte nicht in jedem Fall ermittelt werden. Wir bitten ggfs. um Mitteilung an den Verlag.

Sauf mention contraire, le copyright des œuvres reproduites se trouve chez les photographes qui en sont l'auteur. En dépit de toutes nos recherches, il nous a été impossible d'établir les droits d'auteur dans quelques cas. En cas de réclamation, nous vous prions de bien vouloir vous adresser à la maison d'édition.

FRONT COVER: Photograph by Fernand Fonssagrive. 1959
PAGE 2: Drawing on the deathless theme of the mirror. 1920s

© 2001 TASCHEN GmbH
Hohenzollernring 53, D–50672 Köln
www.taschen.com

Edited by Gilles Néret, Paris
Editorial coordination: Michael Konze, Cologne
Cover design: Angelika Taschen, Cologne
English translation: Sue Rose, London
German translation: Andrea Honecker, Cologne (text);
Bettina Blumenberg, Munich (captions)

Printed in Italy
ISBN 3–8228–1286–2

"Buy them all and add some pleasure to your life."

www.taschen.com

ICONS